FIRE SAFETY

by Lucia Raatma

THE CHILD'S WORLD®
CHANHASSEN, MINNESOTA

The Child's World

Published in the United States of America by the Child's World®
P.O. Box 326, Chanhassen, MN 55317-0326
800-599-READ
www.childsworld.com

*Subject Consultant:
Bridget Clementi,
Safe Kids Coordinator,
Children's Health
Education Center,
Milwaukee, Wisconsin*

Photo Credits: Cover: Corbis; Bettmann/Corbis: 8, 11; Corbis: 5, 6 (Owen Franken), 7, 9, 10, 12 (Volker Mohrke), 12 right (Chase Swift), 15 (Lawrence Manning), 15 right (John Lund), 16 (Craig Lovell), 18, 20 (Tom Stewart), 21 (Robert & Linda Mostyn; Eye Ubiquitous), 22, 25 (Richard Hutchings), 26 (Michael S. Yamashita); Corbis Sygma: 27; Photodisc/Picture Quest: 17; Stockbyte/Punchstock: 18 right.

The Child's World®: Mary Berendes, Publishing Director

Editorial Directions, Inc.: E. Russell Primm, Editorial Director; Elizabeth K. Martin and Katie Marsico, Line Editors; Olivia Nellums, Editorial Assistant; Susan Hindman, Copy Editor; Susan Ashley, Proofreader; Peter Garnham, Fact Checker; Tim Griffin/IndexServ, Indexer; Elizabeth K. Martin and Matthew Messbarger, Photo Researchers and Selectors

Library of Congress Cataloging-in-Publication Data
Raatma, Lucia.
    Fire safety / by Lucia Raatma.
        p. cm. — (Living well)
    Includes bibliographical references and index.
    Contents: Why is fire safety important?—What kind of fires are there?—How can you prevent fires?—How do most fires start?—How can you prepare for a possible fire?—What should you do in case of fire?
    ISBN 1-59296-086-3 (Library Bound : alk. paper)
    1. Fire prevention—Juvenile literature. [1. Fire prevention. 2. Safety.] I. Title. II. Series: Living well (Child's World (Firm))
  TH9148.R32 2004
  628.9'22—dc21   2003006284

TABLE OF CONTENTS

CHAPTER ONE

THE SMOKE ALARM

Dawn was fast asleep in her bed after a long day at school. Suddenly, a sharp beeping noise woke her up. "It can't be morning already," she thought. Then she realized that the noise she heard was not coming from her alarm clock. It was the smoke alarm in the hallway outside her bedroom.

Dawn knew exactly what to do. She jumped out of bed and walked quickly to her bedroom door. She felt the door handle to make sure it was not hot. It was cool. She opened the door carefully and looked into the hallway, but there was no smoke and she did not feel any heat.

For a moment, Dawn thought of going back into her bedroom to get her favorite bear. But she remembered what she had practiced with her family. She left the bear behind and followed the **escape**

route they had planned out of their home. She met her family across the street, at the big tree in front of her neighbor's house. Dawn's dad called the fire department on his cell phone. Firefighters and other **emergency** workers soon arrived to put out the small fire in the family's basement.

Hearing that smoke alarm go off can be very scary. Often, you can prevent some fires from ever happening by following safety rules. But sometimes fires happen, and they can hurt or even kill people. Knowing what to do if there is a fire can help keep you and your family safe.

Firefighters put out the fire in Dawn's basement.

CHAPTER TWO

WHAT KINDS OF FIRES ARE THERE?

Some fires are great. Campfires roast marshmallows and provide good shadows for ghost stories. Fires in fireplaces are warm and make your home cozy. Some people use candles to decorate their homes, and candles are important in many religious traditions. Blazing birthday candles celebrate another year and maybe make wishes come true. Firefighters often start fires in

Not all fire is bad. Without fire, you couldn't enjoy the warmth and coziness of a fireplace.

grasslands or in forests to help prevent bigger fires! They control these fires to make sure they do not spread. These controlled fires can even help seeds grow and make forests healthier. They help to clear dead wood, dried leaves, and plants that can

If forest fires are controlled, they can actually help seeds grow!

turn small fires or lightning strikes into enormous forest fires.

But not all fires are good. In fact, many fires are dangerous. They can burn forests and ruin buildings. They can injure people and leave them without homes. Fires that begin in one place can move on to destroy entire neighborhoods or forests. The Great Chicago Fire of 1871 started in a barn but ended up destroying much of the city. Even fires that should be something good, such as candles on a birthday cake, can turn into something dangerous.

The Great Chicago fire destroyed much of the city in 1871.

CHAPTER THREE

How Do Fires Start?

Fires can start in all sorts of ways. Some fires start with one simple action. For example, some people think that the Great Chicago Fire started when a cow knocked over a lantern in a barn. Other fires start from more complicated problems, such as bad wiring in a building's electrical system.

Many fires start in homes. Some home fires happen when a person falls asleep while smoking or leaves a burning cigarette some-where. Often, they start when people play with matches or

Fires can start when someone falls asleep and leaves a cigarette burning.

lighters. Many home fires begin in the kitchen. **Combustible** items, such as paper, wooden spoons, or even hair and clothes, can catch fire while someone is cooking. Paint or other chemicals can start a fire if they become too hot. Even those pretty lights on a Christmas tree can get too hot and cause a dry tree to burn. Heat

from a **space heater** in an apartment can make a bedspread burst into flames. Then the fire might spread throughout the entire apartment building.

Fires start in other places as well. They might start in the kitchen at school. Someone walking down the street might throw a

It is important to be careful around space heaters because they sometimes cause fires.

lit cigarette into a gutter where there are old newspapers. Forest fires can start when someone leaves a campfire burning. A lightning strike can cause a fire as well. It might seem scary to think about all the different kinds of fires that can happen. But remember, there are things you can do to prevent them from even starting.

Early Firefighters

The first firefighters in North America were not paid. They were volunteers, just like firefighters in some communities are today. They often put out fires with bucket brigades. Members of the fire companies formed long lines. They would fill buckets with water from nearby wells. Then they would pass the buckets up the lines toward the fire.

In 1648, Peter Stuyvesant was the governor of a Dutch settlement that is present-day New York. That year, he started one of the first fire prevention systems. Fire wardens to check for possible fire dangers in the area. Ten years later a group of men kept watch for fires. Today, smoke and fire alarms to the same job.

CHAPTER FOUR

HOW CAN YOU PREVENT FIRES?

There are many ways you can help prevent fires. You can do your part to keep your friends, your family, and yourself safe. The first rule of fire prevention is never to play with matches or lighters. These items are not toys, and they can be very dangerous. If you see matches or lighters lying around, tell an adult.

Always remember that matches and lighters are not toys!

Candles can be pretty, either on a cake or decorating your home. But you should stay away from them when they are lit. They can easily catch your clothing or hair on fire. Only an adult should light candles. When blowing out candles, be careful. Keep your hair back and your clothing out of the way.

You should also be careful not to stand too close to fireplaces or wood stoves. Your clothes could catch fire or you could get burned. If your family uses a space heater, keep it at least 3 feet (1 meter) away from beds, curtains, and other items that can catch fire.

Take a walk around your home with an adult and look for places fires might start. One such danger might be a pile of newspapers or clothes in your basement. These are combustible items that can easily start a larger fire. With an adult, be sure that paint, oil, and other chemicals are stored in the correct containers.

They should not be left in your home. Many communities have rules about disposing of such items. Find out what those rules are, and have an adult get rid of unnecessary chemicals.

If not used properly, electricity can cause fires, too. Never plug more than two things into one electrical **outlet.** Plugging your computer, your lamp, your alarm clock, and your TV in one place makes that outlet work too hard and can cause a fire. Don't play with electrical cords or run them under rugs and carpets. Even when you are playing, don't place blankets or clothes over a lamp. The heat from the light bulb might cause these items to burn.

There are ways to prevent fires in the kitchen, too. Always ask for an adult's help when cooking. Be careful around hot stoves and ovens, especially around oil that is being heated. Oil gets hot quickly and can easily catch fire. Sometimes an oil or grease

Be careful around lighter fluid when someone is grilling (above), and always make sure never to have more than two plugs in an electrical outlet (left).

fire starts in a pot or pan

on the stove.

When cooking outside, keep your

distance from campfires and grills. An adult should always be

watching such fires. Never play with the lighter fluid or other

items used to start these fires. When the cooking is done, make

sure the flame is put out completely.

CHAPTER FIVE

HOW CAN YOU PREPARE
FOR A POSSIBLE FIRE?

It is important to try to prevent fires. But sometimes fires start

anyway, and it is important to know what to do if that happens.

There are many ways to prepare for such an emergency.

At home, ask an adult to keep a **fire extinguisher** in the kitchen. An adult can use this item to quickly put out a small kitchen fire. This keeps a small fire from turning into a big one. You should learn how to use a fire extinguisher, too, just in case you are alone when a small fire starts.

Be prepared by keeping a fire extinguisher in the kitchen.

Remember that water should never be used when trying to put out an oil fire. Water makes the oil splatter and can cause the fire to spread. Instead, an adult can cover the pan of oil with a lid to put out the fire.

Ask an adult to be sure there is a smoke alarm in every room. Smoke alarms, also called smoke detectors, beep very loudly, warning you about smoke in the house. These alarms wake you up if you are sleeping. And they give you time to get out of the house

Smoke alarms will warn you if there is smoke in your house.

before the fire gets worse. Ask an adult to change the batteries in your smoke alarms twice a year. Smoke alarms should be tested regularly. Talk to your family about testing them every month.

It is also important that everyone in your home have an escape route. With your family members, plan two escape routes from every room in the house. Many fires start at night when everyone is asleep, so you should know how to get out of each bedroom. One way out of each room is by the door. But if the door is blocked by fire, you may be able to get out through the windows. For rooms above the first floor, use special plans. One plan is to use an escape ladder to get out a window. An escape ladder is smaller than a normal ladder and can hang out of a window during an emergency. Have an adult show you how they work. Keep one stored where it is easy to find.

If you live in an apartment building, know the fastest route to

the exits, and know the locations of the **fire escapes.** You

should never use elevators during a fire. Instead,

use the stairways or the fire escapes.

In addition to knowing escape

routes, your family should also agree

on a meeting place away from your

*You might have to use a fire escape (above) or an escape ladder (above right)
to leave your home during a fire.*

home. Perhaps it is at the tree across the street or on a neighbor's porch. Choose a spot, and make sure everyone knows where it is.

Several times a year, your family should have fire drills to practice getting out of your home. These drills prepare everyone in case of a fire. It is important to repeat them so everyone remembers their routes. The drills also remind everyone of the rules. Someone in your family should time each drill and see how

A prearranged meeting place could be beneath one of the trees in a neighbor's yard.

long it takes for everyone to get outside to the meeting place.

At school, be sure to follow the rules in fire drills. Listen to your teachers, and learn how to exit the building quickly and safely. The drills are not games. They help you prepare for a fire, and they might even save your life one day.

Today's Firefighters

Firefighters work both in big cities and small towns. Some belong to volunteer companies and work for free. Others are full-time firefighters who get paid. But all of them work hard to prevent fires and to save lives.

To put out fires, these men and women use long hoses that spray water. They also use ladders to reach people trapped by fire. They wear heavy, fireproof clothing and often have to breathe through masks so smoke does not hurt them. Firefighters usually go to fires in big trucks. You can often hear their horns and sirens as they race by.

CHAPTER SIX

WHAT SHOULD YOU
DO IN CASE OF FIRE?

The best advice in case of fire is this: Get out and stay out! If there is

a fire in your home, follow the escape routes you have practiced. Don't

stop to collect toys or other items. Don't try to make a phone call.

Don't even try to put out the fire. Your responsibility is to get out and

If you practice an escape route ahead of time,
you will be prepared if there is an actual fire.

get help. Leave immediately and go to your meeting place. At that point, someone should call 9-1-1 or the local fire emergency number, perhaps from a neighbor's house or from a cell phone.

In some cases, leaving your home when there is a fire might be difficult. For instance, if you are in a room with a door closed, there are other rules you must follow. First, if you see smoke coming in under the door, leave the door closed. Even if you don't see smoke, feel the door and the doorknob. If either is hot, leave the door closed. Seeing smoke or feeling heat means that the fire is near the door.

In such a case, you need to leave the room another way, perhaps through a window. If that is not possible, you need to stay in the room and wait for help. Block the cracks around the door with clothing, blankets, sheets, or anything else you can find to keep smoke from getting into the room. If you have any water, wet a piece of clothing or a towel and hold it over your mouth and nose. This will help to keep you from breathing smoke.

If you do have to wait in a room for help, never hide under a bed or in a closet. Once firefighters are in your home, they will need to find you quickly, so make sure they can see you. If you have a phone in that room, call 9-1-1 or your local emergency number and stay put. If there is a window in the room, but you cannot leave through it, open it and stand in front of it. The fresh air will help you breathe. And firefighters will be able to spot you easily.

If you are in a room with a door closed but you don't see smoke or feel heat, open the door very slowly. If you then feel heat or if smoke pours in, close the door quickly and stay behind it. If not, then use your escape route. Move quickly, but do not run. Smoke rises in the air, so the safest air is near the ground. It is important to stay low, below the smoke. Inhaling smoke can hurt you as much as the fire can. So get on your hands and knees, and crawl your way out of your home.

If at some point your clothing catches fire, do not run! Running actually gives the fire more air and makes the flames burn faster. Instead of running—stop. Immediately drop to the ground and roll

Once a fire starts, a building can burn quickly. It is important to get out as fast as possible.

around. The rolling will cut off the air and put out the flames. In your fire drills, practice this with your family. Remind them and yourself: Stop, drop, and roll.

Once you have safely left the house or building, go to your meeting place and stay there. Do not go back inside for any reason. If anyone in your family is not at the meeting place, let firefighters know. Tell them what room the family member was in. But never try to rescue anyone yourself.

If a fire starts at your school, follow your teacher's directions. Remember what you have learned in fire drills, and leave the building calmly but quickly. If a fire starts when you are in a building you are not familiar with, look for exit signs. Listen for any announcements that are being made and follow those directions. Just as in apartment buildings, you should never take an elevator during a fire. Instead, always use the stairs.

When you are leaving a building that is on fire, it is important to move quickly and stay calm. Whatever you do, don't panic! Remember the rules you have learned and trust yourself. That's the best way to stay safe from fire.

Always use the stairs during a fire. Never take the elevator.

Glossary

combustible (kuhm-BUHSS-tuh-buhl) Something that is combustible catches on fire easily.

emergency (i-MUR-juhn-see) An emergency is a sudden and dangerous situation that requires immediate attention.

escape route (ess-KAPE ROOT) An escape route is a planned way to leave a building in case of emergency.

fire escapes (FIRE ess-KAPES) Fire escapes are sets of metal stairs on the outsides of buildings. They are used to leave a building in case of fire.

fire extinguisher (FIRE ek-STING-gwish-ur) A fire extinguisher is a metal container than holds chemicals used to put out a fire.

outlet (OUT-let) An outlet is a place where appliances and other machines can be plugged in to get electricity.

space heater (SPAYSS HEE-tur) A space heater is a small heating unit that can be moved from room to room.

Questions and Answers about Fire Safety

On TV, heroes are always running into burning buildings and saving people. Can't I do that, too? No! Those people are actors, and the fires are not real. Only trained firefighters and emergency workers should enter a building that is on fire.

How many smoke alarms should be in my home? Ideally, there should be one in every room. If that is not possible, there should be at least one on each floor and outside the bedrooms.

Is it okay to leave space heaters on or candles burning when I leave a room? No. Always turn off heaters when you are not using them. And never leave burning candles unattended.

Should I call 9-1-1 the minute I suspect a fire? No. It is important to get out of the building first and then to call for help.

Helping a Friend Learn about Fire Safety

▶ At school, talk to your friends about fire drills. If anyone makes jokes about the drills, tell them fire drills are important and can save lives.

▶ Help your friends plan escape routes in their own homes. Encourage them to have fire drills with their own families.

▶ Remind your friends to have smoke alarms in their homes. Encourage them to test the alarms regularly and remember to change the batteries.

▶ Practice two parts of your escape route with your friends. First, crawl low under the smoke. Next, practice stopping, dropping, and rolling as though your clothing were on fire. Practicing can seem silly. But the more you practice, the better prepared you will be!

Did You Know?

▶ There is an easy way to remember to change the batteries in your smoke alarms. Your family can do it twice a year, each time you change your clocks for daylight savings time in the spring and in the fall.

▶ A smoke alarm can "smell" a fire long before your nose can.

▶ During a fire, you should never enter a smoke-filled stairwell or hallway. Find another way out.

▶ Firefighters often give talks about fire safety. Maybe your teacher can ask a local firefighter to visit your class.

How to Learn More about Fire Safety

At the Library: Nonfiction
Chaiet, Donna, and Francine Russell. *The Safe Zone.* New York: Morrow Junior Books, 1998.

Gutman, Bill. *Harmful to Your Health.* New York: Twenty-First Century Books, 1996.

Sanders, Pete, and Steve Myers. *Personal Safety.* Brookfield, Conn.: Copper Beech Books, 1999.

Schwartz, Linda. *What Would You Do? A Kid's Guide to Tricky and Sticky Situations.* Santa Barbara, Calif.: Learning Works, 1990.

Silverstein, Alvin, Virginia Silverstein, and Laura Silverstein Nunn. *Staying Safe.* Danbury, Conn.: Franklin Watts, 2000.

At the Library: Fiction
Beatty, Monica Driscoll. *Fire Night!* Santa Fe, N.M.: Health Press, 1998.

Brown, Marc. *Arthur's Fire Drill.* New York: Random House, 2000.

On the Web
Visit our home page for lots of links about fire safety:
http://www.childsworld.com/links.html

Note to Parents, Teachers, and Librarians: We routinely verify our Web links to make sure they're safe, active sites—so encourage your readers to check them out!

Through the Mail or by Phone
American Red Cross National Headquarters
431 18th Street, N.W.
Washington, DC 20006
202/303-4498

National Center for Injury Prevention and Control
4770 Buford Highway, N.E.
Atlanta, GA 30341
770/488-1506

National Fire Protection Association
1 Batterymarch Park
Quincy, MA 02269
617/770-3000

National SAFE KIDS Campaign
1301 Pennsylvania Avenue, N.W.
Suite 100
Washington, DC 20004
202/662-0600

National Safety Council
1121 Spring Lake Drive
Itasca, IL 60143
630/285-1121

The Nemours Center for Children's Health Media
Alfred I. duPont Hospital for Children
1600 Rockland Road
Wilmington, DE 19803
302/651-4046

U.S. Consumer Product Safety Commission
Washington, DC 20207
800/638-2772

Index

About the Author

Lucia Raatma received her bachelor's degree in English literature from the University of South Carolina and her master's degree in cinema studies from New York University. She has written a wide range of books for young people. When she is not researching or writing, she enjoys going to movies, practicing yoga, and spending time with her husband, their daughter, and their golden retriever. She lives in New York.